Textures

MILO EDUCATIONAL BOOKS & RESOURCES

www.miloeducationalbooks.com

E. Cardenas

N. Delgado

Published by:

 **EDUCATIONAL BOOKS & RESOURCES**

www.miloeducationalbooks.com
P.O. Box 41353, Houston, Texas 77241-1353
Phone: (888) 640-MILO & (713) 466-MILO
Fax: (888) 641-MILO & (713) 896-MILO

Textures written by E. Cardenas & N. Delgado

ISBN-13:   978-1-60698-045-3   Paperback
               978-1-60698-046-0   Six-pack paperback
               978-1-60698-047-7   Big book paperback

Library of Congress Control Number: 2008905754

First Edition

Printed in China

Visit our website at **www.miloeducationalbooks.com** for more information and resources for students, teachers, and parents.

Credits:

Front cover & page 1: © 2006 Norma Cornes/ShutterStock, Inc.; Back cover: © 2006 David Crippen (left) & Gary Unwin (right)/ShutterStock, Inc.; Pages 3 (top left) & 4-5: © 2006 karen roach/ShutterStock, Inc.; Pages 3 (top center) & 6-7: © 2006 Elena Elisseeva/ShutterStock, Inc.; Pages 3 (top right) & 8-9: © 2006 Allyson Ricketts/ShutterStock, Inc.; Pages 3 (bottom left) & 10-11: © 2006 Alex Balako/ShutterStock, Inc.; Pages 3 (bottom center) & 12-13: © 2006 Lori Martin/ShutterStock, Inc.; Pages 3 (bottom right) & 14-15: © 2006 Jeff R. Clow/ShutterStock, Inc.; Page 16 from left to right & top to bottom: © 2006 Ximagination, Todd Hackwelder, Petr Vaclavek, Chris Gjersvik, VTupinamba, & Jim Lopes/ShutterStock, Inc.

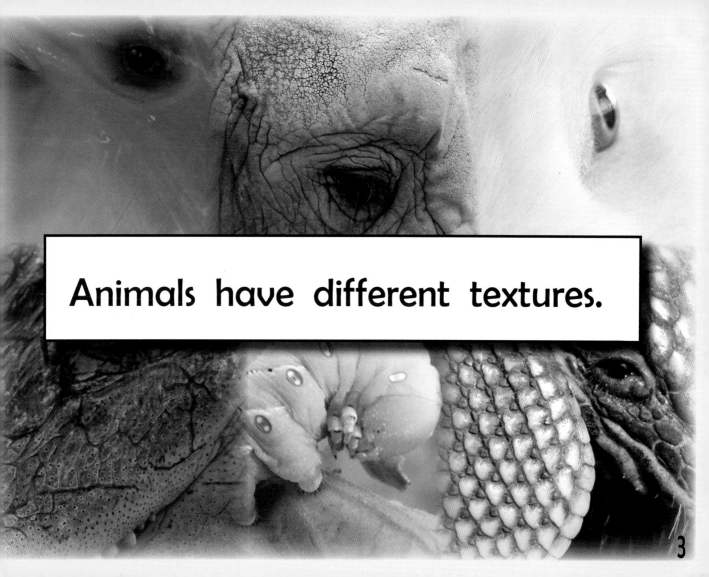

Animals have different textures.

3

A dolphin's skin
is smooth,

4

but an elephant's skin
is coarse.

7

A rabbit's fur
is fluffy,

8

but a crocodile's skin is rough.

A worm's skin
is soft,

12

but an armadillo's skin
is hard.

What textures do these animals have?